The World Through My Eyes

Cabiria Aquarius

BookLeaf Publishing

Presentation by *BookLeaf Publishing*

Web: www.bookleafpub.com

E-mail: info@bookleafpub.com

ISBN: 9789395755832

First edition 2023

DEDICATION

To Andy Krieter

For choosing me as your favourite poet amongst plenty of established and well-versed laureates. For believing in me when I was still learning to believe in myself.

Thank you.

ACKNOWLEDGEMENT

So many people in my life made this possible. Thank you, Bookleaf publishing, for having this challenge. A way to challenge myself and my writing and to prove to myself I can do this.
Thank you to my Bookleaaf consultant and my editor for helping me on this journey of making this the best it can be.
Thank you to my mother Kathy Plamondon, for allowing me to chase my dreams and believing in me.
Thank you to Caitlin Mehew, Abby Grundy, Jade Gibbs, Britt Samples, Jodie Callen, Taylor Leszczynski, Amber Davis, Erin Farmer, Alexandra Wilkerson, and Trevor Long, for being there for me and believing in me and pushing me throughout the times you've all known me for.
Thank you to mother nature and life for being my inspiration.

People Are

People are like writer's block
I. Don't have time or motivation to write (I don't have any ideas)
II. So many ideas but don't know where to start (doesn't know which one to focus on)
III. So many ideas but isn't in the mood to write (fear of not getting it right, so doesn't start)
People are like writer's block

People are like butterflies
A caterpillar finds a way to be protected and feeds until it can't anymore
It's learning how to exist
How to live
It will wrap itself in a cocoon ready to be molded into who it's going to be
Taking in information
Finalizing who it's going to be
It's ready
Cocoon cracks
A butterfly emerges and spreads its wings
A rainbow of colours
A different pattern on each one

It knows who it is now
It's flying free
Being who it's supposed to be
Chasing who they want to be
People are like butterflies

People are like the ocean
I. Sunny day, calm and shiny waters
You love sitting and surrounding yourself in the calm
Staring out into the calm blue just breathing
II. Cool breezes and surfing waves
You laugh and have fun
Can't wait to go back and have fun
III. A cloud appears, a storm, the waters rage
You wonder where the cloud came from
Wonder if you'll survive the storm
People are like the ocean

But most importantly

People are like people
We have our flaws
Our strengths and weaknesses
Our similarities and differences
Celebrate who we are
In all our shapes and colours
Celebrate who we want to be

There will be those who prove that humanity is a beautiful thing
There will be those who would like nothing more than to see their peers go down a few pegs

I've always been fascinated by people
And stories
Each culture has a story
Each person has a story

The world can't be black and white
It comes in shades of grey
Without the bad
Would we appreciate the good?

Be proud of who you are
Show the world your wings
And if they look weird
Shine Brighter
The world needs weird

People are like people

Sonder

It costs \$0 to be kind
You don't know how their life could be
So many different people so many lives blow my mind
It's amazing, don't you agree?

On the train surrounded by different faces
That I've never seen
Going on their way to different places
They might be nice they might be mean

I'll never know who they are
What they do who they know
What are their emotional scars?
How did they grow?

They are a footnote on my way
And yet I find myself wondering about
What do they do in their day to day
Are they happy? Do they doubt?

What are their hopes and dreams?
I hope they reach them
I hope they have good support teams
Do they know they are a gem?

People can do amazing things
And people can think up no good plans
I hope they grow their wings
What's with all these bans?

The world is a beautiful place
What wonders can be found today?
The world is a scary space
What do you have to say?

What's your life like?
Who are your family and friends?
I like to walk and take out my bike
When you look at the world - you use which
lens?

What thoughts and feelings go through your
mind?
Where are you going - what's your routine?
How do you see mankind?
Do you feel seen?

I don't know who you are
I hope you're doing okay
Know that you are a star
I hope you find your way

Butterfly Effect

A butterfly will flap its wings
And a choice elsewhere will be made
It’s a tornado - you hear as the alarm rings
You huddle in the shelter wondering and afraid

A butterfly will flap its wings
You decide on your life path
With different theories and strings
You know the language of science and math

A butterfly will flap its wings
And suddenly you’re stepping outside your
routine zone
Going to an orchestra performance - pulls at
your heartstrings
Your mind is blown

A butterfly will flap its wings
You say something to someone
To them, it stings
They will do anything to show they’ve won

A butterfly's wings will flap
You decide to embrace your strange
It happened slowly then with a zap

Time for you to allow change

A butterfly's wings will flap
Things will change as you grow older
It will feel like a trap
You will get bolder

A butterfly's wings will flap
Things will not be the same
Younger you didn't like them but now time for a nap
Some nights will be wild and some will be tame

A butterfly's wings will flap
Time to show the world what you've got
You've been given a tap-on
Take that spot-light

A butterfly's wings will flap
Some days you will feel strong
Others you'll just want to curl up in someone's lap
You've got this, you'll find your way along

A butterfly will flap its wings
We think we take our chances
It's all connected on strings
The world is holding, making us do dances

Roses

The first step is planting a seed
What do you want to be?
The next step is giving it sunshine
Are you sure that's what you want?
Okay
Now time to water it
Learn about that path in depth
Continue to water it
You continue to learn
You might not see progress right away
Don't give up
Look there's a sprout!
Time to water it some more
Keep learning
And eventually
You'll see the stem
You know enough
To have a grip
On knowledge
Keep watering
Eventually
You'll see
More progress
You'll see
From a seed

To a sprout
To a stem
There are leaves
There's the bud
You know so much
Time to bloom
Those petals are so pretty
You are doing amazing
The world will see your petals
They won't see how you came
To be so beautiful
They will judge your petals
Without thinking of your thorns
They will judge your thorns
Forgetting how beautiful your petals are
But a rose isn't a rose
Without petals and thorns
It's a risky beauty
And darling
So are you
Don't you forget that
You are a rose

Blue

Words fall from lips and as the words sink
in they find their target-your heart- shoulders sag and
spirits fall as you wonder why you try at all.
Your mood is low as you sulk in the words,
wondering
where you could've failed. What could have gone
better? You are alone in a room and the
tears begin to fall and you don't know
what to do. Smiles are nowhere to be found and
struggling to
come around. You don't know where
to go from here. Your mind replays the words spoken
by someone dear
wondering what you did wrong to
deserve these words. How could you prove
them wrong? That's not the best way to
do things but you feel like you're losing. Blue is the
emotion
You feel as the wave of
Sadness and loneliness take
you away you don't know how to crawl
Out of the well of emotions you've
Found yourself in
The weight is heavy and won't lift
You try
To find a smile
Where you usually do

It’s not working
Time to let the weight get heavier
Listen to sad music
At least you know it understands
Where you are
Where you’ve been
You try and go for a walk under the endless
Blue of the sky and the
Breeze ruffles your hair and tickles your
Skin you feel relaxed
Once again
You go for a swim
The calm blue water
Washes your worries away
You find your smile again
You don’t need their approval
Only your own
Chase your dreams
You have it in you
Just have to believe and
You're halfway there you’ve
Made it through the hard
Part and now to push through
You are you
Don’t let anyone push you
Down
Back into that
Blue

Dance

Deep breath
Press play
Let the music take you away
Thump
Thump
Thump
Your mind focused
On the steps
The beat
Thump
Thump
Thump
The lyrics
The way your body moves
How the music makes you feel
Thump
Thump
Thump
Your mind serene
As you spin on your heel
The audience enraptured
As you set the scene
Thump
Thump
Thump

Exhilaration
As you feel the sheen of sweat
Drip down your brow
Hoping it's not visible
Thump
Thump
Thump
You twirl and spin
Telling a story
With your body
No words
Leave your lips
You are a silent
storyteller
Thump
Thump
Thump
Colourful costumes
Each chosen for a reason
Every detail
Thought out
Thump
Precise
Thump
Hairstyle
Jewelry
Colours
Design
Thump

Thump
Thump
Such a thrill
It ends way too quickly
You come to a standstill
Pose as you were told
As you are the mold
Thump
You bow at the curtain call
A large grin on your face
Hoping you brought magic and joy to all

Eyes

Eyes are the doorway to the soul
The way you can tell if a smile is real or not
It will change on any given day if their wall is up or down
If you know someone well you'll know the signs

They will sparkle and gleam in excitement
Or dull and void when sad and alone
When talking about their dreams they will shine bright
Or guarded if they had a bad day

Blues greens and browns are colours we see
Each unique to each person we know
Each matches different grounds of the planet
That can all be found at a beach if you look around

Everyone loves looking into ocean blues
Or blues that look like the sky
As bright as a brand new day
That's nice to take a hike at the lake

Then there are the forest greens
Or shine like an emerald
That you can stare at for hours
Which is completely fine of course

Don't forget the chocolate browns
Or nice wood for a good campfire
Your attention is caught in a net and won't be let go
You only ever want more of their warmth

Within these colours three
There is quite the variety
Bringing you to your knees all these hues are
Don't want to let them out of your sight for a moment

There will never be enough words
To describe what each set looks like
Looking at them with glee is all we know
The confidence to strut with eyes smiling pulls us

Of course, everyone has their preference
Of which colour eyes calls to them more
As long as they are smiling like the sun on any given day
I think you'd find it difficult to despise any combination

Eyes are the doorway to the soul
What you might find is up to you
Willing to stay long enough to find out
What lies deep in the mind of those you know

Love

What is love?
Love isn’t anger
Fighting and bickering every night
Arguing over mistakes made
That can easily be fixed
Love is understanding that
Mistakes happen and looking
To fix it together and now
Having a story to laugh at
Later because life is colourful

What is love?
Love isn’t planning a family trip
Without the family’s input and
Hoping they’ll just be happy
And grateful the entire time
Love is asking everyone involved
What they’d like to see and making
It happen together. Finding compromises
If one party doesn’t like something requested
And knowing and learning about each other

What is love?
Love is making sure you both

Have time to chase your dreams
No matter what, take turns or
At the same time and see each
Other when you can because love
Shouldn't be about just one of you
Finding what you want and the other
Stuck doing things they don't enjoy
Love is not being beholden to someone
And being your own person

What is love?
Love isn't controlling
You are allowed to go to school
And take whichever classes you want or need
You are allowed to wear what makes
You happy and confident in your own skin
Love shouldn't demand you change your clothes
Love shouldn't tell you not to take a certain
class
Love is supportive and kind
Love is admiring you for who you are, not
What you wear or insecure to not let you
Show yourself off

What is love?
Love is communication
Always making sure you're on the
Same page so there are no
Misunderstandings

Talking together is key
Learning about one another is key
Key to falling in love
Staying in love
Being in love

What is love?
Love is funny
Laughing together at different
Shenanigans you both get up to
Either separately or together
Laughing at jokes you tell each other
Finding a reason to smile
Together
Love isn't silence

What is love?
Love is also silence together
They are doing their thing
You're doing your thing
Maybe in the same room
Maybe not
Enjoying each other's company
Living life how you both enjoy
Together on your own
Maybe the occasional glance at
The other
Love is not silence all the time
Spending time together is

Why you are with them
So spend time together
But being your own person
Is important too

What is love?
Love is supportive
Love isn't there to
Change who you are
What you like
They are there to
Take you as you are
With what you like
They can't tell you
Who to be
What to like
They chose you
Then you shouldn't
Need to change

What is love?
Love is kind
Love takes care of you
When you're sick
Wants to make you happy
When you are sad
Love doesn't look the other way
Love gives you love
Because they love you

What is love?
Love isn't caring more
About the welfare of
Objects more than your
Welfare
Objects are replaceable
Expensive maybe depending
But replaceable
People are one of a kind
All around
They are irreplaceable

What is love?
Love is real
Love is two sided
Not one that's always
Taking
Love is work
It won't always be
Easy
If you want it
You have to work
At it always
To be happy
Find who you will be
Fits with who they
Will be
Love is real

Not fake to pull
Away once they got you
Love will
choose you
Everyday

What is love?
Love isn't blind
Love sees you for all that you are
And loves you
Flaws included
Every puzzle
Piece of you
Love sees you
And smiles

Love is
And isn't
A lot of things
To different people
But love will always
Should always
Be real
What that looks like
For you
Only you
Can find that
Out

Music

Feel the drum
Beat
In your bones

Feel the energy
Hype
In the air

Hear the lyrics
Reach
Your heart

Hear the excitement
In
Your ears

Music allows us
Connection
With others

Feel the
Emotions
In your veins

Feel the
Beat
In your step

Feel the energy
Hype
In your bones

Sway to the
Melody
In your ears

Your mind thinks of
Life
As the lyrics play

Songs make you
Happy
Dance around the house

Songs make you
Sad
Cry in your room

Music gives you
Memory
As lyrics hit home

Music brings you

Fun
Dance with your friends

Remember when
Music
Was there

Certain songs bring
Memories
Of moments of life

Moments you wish to
Hold
Onto

Moments you wish to
Let
Go of

Life is never
Dull
When music is on

Road trips and singalongs
Fun
With friends and family

Chords and quartets play
Symphonies

At the theatre

Country rock and
Jazz
Too

Music has something
For
Everyone

Showtunes and game tunes
Bring
Happiness too

Violin piano and
Guitars
Have sway

English French
Italian
As well

Music can be
Anything
You want it to be

Nights in nights
Out
Music can be anywhere

Dance around your
Kitchen
On your own

Singalong with your
Friends
Laughing the night away

Music on your way to
Work
Going about routine

Buskers trying to give
You
A smile

Music to try to
Save
Themselves from poverty

Music so
Life
Isn't so quiet

Crickets and birds
Music
To our ears too

Mother Nature gives us
Music
Everywhere

Rushing waterfalls
Splashing
Is music

Firewood
Crackling
As a campfire

Birds
Chirping
On the branches

Spoons on
Pots
Make their beat

A baby's
Laugh
Is a precious sound

Voice and laughter of
Loved ones
Are things you like to hear

There's music in
Silence
Part of the dance

The way
Words
Fall from lips

Car horns on the
Road
Can be a symphony

Books going back on
Shelves
Sliding into place

The click of the
Camera
Capturing moments forever

Music can be
Anything
Anywhere you look

Fire

Fire is a candle
A light in the dark
A way to see what's been taken away
Fire is a candle
To stare into
A little wick of heat
Fire is a candle
Spreading a lovely scent into the air
To bring a smile to your face

Fire is a stovetop
Boiling water to make pasta
Feed your pasta addiction
Fire is a stovetop
Hard boiling, scrambling eggs
Or over easy
Or a nice omelet
Fire is a stovetop
Stir-fry or soup tonight?
Let's have some food

Fire is a fireplace
Giving you heat when you are cold
Fire is a fireplace
Wood crackling for a nice aesthetic

Fire is a fireplace
To make makeshift s’mores

Fire is fireworks
Light up the dark sky
Blasts of colour
Fire is fireworks
Celebrating certain days of the year
Fire is fireworks
Fun night with friends
For a brief moment
In time
Fire is fireworks
Poor kitties and doggies' ears
Hurt from the
booms

Fire is a campfire
Sit around talking with friends and family
Fire is a campfire
Roasting marshmallows
Don’t burn it!
Oh, that’s part of the fun
Roasting hotdogs too
Fire is a campfire
A nice night at the campsite

Fire is a house fire
Catching and spreading to

Every room
Fire is a house fire
Eating your entire life
Into nothing
You start anew

Fire is anger
Fire is rage
Life isn't going your way
You scream and curse
Fire is anger
Fire is rage
Someone's done you wrong
Your only solution to
Be frustrated and mad
And cause pain

Fire is a forest fire
Trees burning
Grass catching
Fire is a forest fire
Nothing left
Unscathed
Fire is destruction
Fire is a forest fire
Burning down so the world
Can start anew

Fire is a phoenix
Born from the ashes
Its life will start
Back at the beginning

Fire is destruction and pain yet
Fire is life and warmth
There are two sides to every coin
There are two sides to fire
It is a fragile candle flame
Strong house fire
Warm campfire
Angry forest fire
Fire isn't just
Pain
Fire is
Life again
Start fresh
Fire is beautiful destruction

Earth

Earth is a grain of sand
So tiny you can't hold a single grain
As many as you can hold
Easily
Slip through your fingers
Earth is a grain of sand
More grains than we can count
Underneath our feet
Keeping us on land

Earth is a pebble
Getting stuck in our sandals
Coming with us wherever we go
Until we stop to pick it out
Earth is a pebble
So many pathways

Earth is a rock
Time to skip rocks across the lake
How many skips did you get?
Earth is a rock
Some too heavy to lift

Earth is a boulder
Keeping us from walking forward

Can't be budged
Earth is a boulder
Which way should we go now?

Earth is the land we stand on
The ground we walk on
Everywhere

Earth is the soil
We plant seeds in
We garden in
Earth is the soil
We cherish

Earth is the trees
We get air from
The flowers we smile at
The strength we need
To stand on our feet

Earth is determination
To chase dreams
Be who we are
Earth is strength
Where we feel weak
To keep going
Good things are
Just around
The corner

Earth is beauty
Gorgeous natural
Landscapes
Each country
Has nature
We take
For granted

Earth is home
For animals in
The wild
Earth is nature
Circle of life
On a daily basis

Earth is this planet
The name of the place
We all call home
Earth is this planet
That we've been
Mistreating
Polluting
Littering
On
Earth is this planet
We take for granted
It's time we
Save it

Save the
People
On it
Save each other
Save
Ourselves
Earth is this planet
It’s time to
Love it
As it’s
Loved us

Air

Air is the breath
We take
The breath
We let go
The breath
We hold

Air is a light breeze
You feel in the
Shade on a hot day
Air is a light breeze
On a mild day
On a nice walk

Air is a gust
Strong near the sea
Whipping your hair
All over your face

Air is the wind
Giving you goosebumps
All over your skin

Air is the wind
In a storm

Pushing you back
As you walk to
Home or
Safety
Air is the wind
Strong enough
To pick you up
Toss you over
Air is the wind
Strong enough
To uproot trees
That damages
Houses

Air is a tornado
That will pickup
Or
Destroy
Whatever is in
It's path

Air is excitement
Energy you feel
At a concert
Air is excitement
You feel for
Aspects in your
Life

Air is joy
Nice day
Nice breeze
Good things
Going on
Air is joy
You feel more
Than happy
Life is
Good

Air is calm
Peaceful
Just what you need
Air is unbalanced
Can pull you every
Which way

Air is impatient
Air is our
Breath
The oxygen
We breathe in
The dioxide
We breathe out

Air is part
Of what
Keeps us
Here

Air is
What we need
Yet
Air can
Destroy us
In a
Heartbeat

Air is
life

Water

Water is a raindrop
Falling from the sky
The sky is crying
Water is a raindrop
Cleansing
Preparing to start anew

Water is in a glass
Stay hydrated
To stay alive
Water is in a glass
Is it half empty
Or
Is it half full

Water is a shower
Clean yourself
Stay fresh
Water is a shower
Wash your stress away

Water is a bath
Relax
Take care of your body
Water is a bath
Have Epsom salts
Take care of your mental health

Water is a pond
Fish swim
Back and forth
Water is a pond
Calm waters

Water is a lake
Beware lake Superior
If the wind is strong
Water is a lake
Go swim
You'll freeze your butt

Water is a stream
Running beside you
In the park

Water is a flood
Water along the streets
Swim or float
Water is a flood
Damaging what you know

Water is a tsunami
Large waves
No one can serf
Water is a tsunami
Get to higher ground

Water is calm
Water is collected
Refreshing

And clear

Water is fun
Laying at the beach
Playing in the serf
As the waves come and go

Water is a pool
Swimming laps
On your own
Water is a pool
Diving techniques
With friends
Water is a pool
Poolside party
With family

Water is life
Drink it
Swim it
Wash stress away
Life
Death
Find life again
So many
Creatures
Call
Water
Their home

Spirit

The world knows the four elements of time
Fire earth air and water make the world go
The fifth one has been forgotten - what crime
Spirit is the most important one though

High or low spirit keeps the world afloat
Spirit is a zest for life if you will
Someone with low spirit may sink their boat
High spirit folks are up for any thrill

Energy to take care of each other
Keeping spirits high spread love all around
Being surrounded by our earth mother
Having fun with friends making quite a sound

Spirit is all around us in the air
Something that cannot be seen yet is there

Winter

At the stroke of midnight
No moon visible in the dark sky
Snow decided to take flight
The flakes invisible to the naked eye

Time for the earth to go to sleep
For the cycle of life to start again
The snow wants to be steep
Watching it fall gives a certain zen

Winter means cold
The earth won't yield crops
Time to gather what food you can hold
Though you can continue to check shops

The earth is dull and bare
However a certain beauty can still be found
Snow has a shine you just want to stare
As it falls to the ground

Winter shows beauty in death
And to bloom it will be good to begin anew
It's always well to think and take a breath
Helps you figure out what to do

Winter is cold however there are so many
activities to choose
Skating skiing sledding if outside you wish
Or a few inside if you find too many a bruise
A fire and a cup of hot cocoa with your dish

Snowball fights building snowmen, snow angels
too
Snuggling under a blanket with a good book
Staring out the window with the view
Playing and dancing to music as you cook

Fun and beautiful yet cold and cruel
Winter shows both sides of life
Time to enjoy yule
Cut the yule log with a good knife

Spring

The snow is melting away
The trees are regrowing their leaves and waking
The sun is giving more warmth everyday
You are no longer cold and shaking

Flowers blooming everywhere
The beach a common trip site
It is now allergy season you swear
Anything could be your blight

Going for a nice walk
Feeling a sweet breeze on your face
With a friend having a talk
In the pretty open space

Beautiful sunrises and good days
Venturing outside more
Getting glorious sun rays
When you step out the door

The earth is being reborn
Animals are waking up now
On this fine morn
To go looking for chow

Let's go for a hike
On a trail
Did you want to bring your bike?
On reaching the end we release a large exhale

The world is colourful once more
No longer dull and white
Going outside is no longer a chore
Days are looking bright

Flowers and butterflies and bees
A nice breeze and good sun
Leaves regrowing on trees
Exploring outdoors is a ton of fun

Summer

The noonday sun high in the sky
The heat like fire on your skin
Your mind constantly asking why
The sun's decided to grin

Go outside and play
Swim at the beach
Have some ice cream today
Look at your face beam

Time for vacation
Where are you going to go?
First stop is the train station
From there you don't know

The heat is so crazy you sweat
All you want to do is be inside with the AC
Or dive in a pool but not yet
You aren't yet free

Plans piled on plans piled on plans
It's always go go go
Always something in your hands
But sometimes just go with the flow

Trips and fun times
Smiles and laughter
Spending so many dimes
Making memories for after

As time starts to pass
Wishing you could go back
Replaying the memories, fragile as glass
Hoping you don’t crack

The sun is sinking
The chill is coming
Felt a lot like just quick blinking
The time for classes is incoming

Autumn

The sun is setting
The air is cool
You are no longer sweating
Grab a sweater, don't be a fool

Time for pumpkin spice
Leaves are changing colour and falling down
Don't forget everything nice
No need to frown

School is on
Stress is about to begin
Where has the summer gone?
You get worn thin

The scary month is here
Halloween enthusiasts grin
They do not easily feel fear
They will be crazy every min-ute

The streams in the park
With the colourful leaves on the ground
The scratchy tree bark
In the quiet is a nice sound

The earth is slowly dying
Training us to feel the crisp air
No need for any crying
It isn't a scare

Water begins turning to ice
As time marches ever on
To some it is considered nice
The land giving a yawn

With the air getting crispy
We give thanks
The wind making our hair wispy
We gather our ranks

The earth is turning white
Time for the cycle to restart
Everything will be alright
Carry on with a good heart

Yellow

All I see is the yellow sun
As I grin at what my life has to offer
So many fun adventures
And memories
Taken in everyday
The world is showing me
What I've been missing
What I needed
Things left
And things gained
The sun is shining
I have so much to live for
Everyday isn't the same
Yet
I have a smile
I will get through
Whatever storms
Will come to
Me
I am not
Alone
I have
A great
Support system
Around me

They will
Be right
Beside me
With me
For anything
I need
They make me
Smile
Laugh
And have fun
So many
Smiles
And so much
Laughter
Some
Tears of course
But
The sun comes shining through
I'm finding it easier
Day by day
To believe in myself
Seeing my worth
Is a
Beautiful
Thing
And
Knowing I
Am worthy
Of

Taking up
Space
On this planet
On this earth
In the lives
Of those
That choose
To be
By
My side
I have their backs
And they have mine
I will forever be
Grateful
To them
All
They are
Why
I smile
As well as
The little things
In life
Like flowers
And butterflies
And the bright blue sky
Pools to swim in
Books to read
Music to take me to another place
Each beat

Of my
Heart
Letting me know
I'm alive
And well
Family
That makes me laugh
Friends that believe in me
A love that keeps me
Safe
Friends that see
My potential
My smiles
And love
Being around me
Talking with me
Trees are cool
Different types
And leaves
Fall changes their colours
And I
Breathe the air
Love going for walks
And animals are a thing
That exists
They are so fun
Most of them
When I think of the world I'm in
I see yellow

And all sorts of other colours
I am happy
Most of the time
I give my love
To me and
To those in my life
When I can
Plants
And movies
And children
Too
Give me hope
That maybe
Things will get much better
Soon
Cooking and
Baking
Food and
Dessert
Are fun to eat
If you know what
You want
Time is a funny thing
It keeps on going
And yet
While I wish I could
Go back
To some
Things

I can’t wait
To see
Where time
Will take
Me
I am the sun
Shining in life
I hope
You see
The light
In your tunnel
Too

Cameras

Click
Goes the camera
As a memory
Is captured
Kept on a screen
Forever after
To look back on
In the rain
If that is what you
Wish

Flash
Goes the light
Because maybe
It’s too dark
Without it
As you attempt
Your best
To capture
Memories
In the dark
Doing your best
To grab
Onto
What you are experiencing

To look back on
On a rainy day

Swish
Goes the camera
On your wrist
Or your neck
As you walk
Waiting for the perfect
Moment
To lift it to your
Eyes
To capture
A moment
In time
Perhaps a memory
Perhaps a moment
That's right in front of you
A beautiful glance of a waterfall
A tree branch with a bird
A bear cub following it's
Mama
A single
Leaf
Hanging on
Breaks
And falls
A single
Water drop

As it falls from
The sky

Bump
Your camera goes
Against your
Chest
Stomach
Arm
As you walk
Searching for that
One perfect
Shot
You don't know
What you're looking for
But you'll know
When you find it

There are
Different types
Of cameras
There are those
Electric ones
You can see
The results
Right away
Which can be nice
But there is another feeling entirely
If you need

A
Dark room

The negatives
Splash
In the fluids of the
Chemicals
As they load
What you captured
To the surface
Showing you
Maybe you made
A mistake
The angle is
Wrong
But maybe
You
Clicked
The shutter
Just
At the right
Time
And your
Breath
Catches
As you see
The image
Slowly
Come

Forward

Cameras allow
Memories
That you may
Forget
Have a way
To come back
Or memories you know well
To have visual companions
They are
Magic
To me

Words

Words are
Powerful
Things

Once said
They cannot
Be taken
Back

Think
Before you
Speak

Words can be used
To praise and cherish
They can also be used
To create fear and harm

Never underestimate
What your words
Do to those you say them
To

Only takes a moment to say
However to those you say them to

Lasts a lifetime
Of love
Or fear
Of happiness
Or despair

I choose
To give words
Of love
Cherishing
Those around me
Using my words
To hold
Them near
As they are so
Dear

Others have used them
To bring fear
Believing they are just
Helping
And yet
Brings harm

Or maybe
Words that are said
Weren't thought to be either
And yet
Caused happiness

Or harm
To those around

Words and actions
Same yet different
Do your words echo your actions?
Do your actions echo your words?
Do your words cause tears or smiles?

Words
Are beautiful
Words
Are pain
Words have the power
To change
The world
If we let them

www.ingramcontent.com/pod-product-compliance
Lightning Source LLC
LaVergne TN
LVHW021139181025
823732LV00040B/429
9789395755832